Your first 100 words in

PERSIAN

Persian for Total Beginners Through Puzzles and Games

Series concept
Jane Wightwick

Illustrations
Mahmoud Gaafar

Persian edition
Abdi Rafiee

McGraw·Hill

New York   Chicago   San Francisco   Lisbon   London   Madrid   Mexico City
Milan   New Delhi   San Juan   Seoul   Singapore   Sydney   Toronto

Library of Congress Cataloging-in-Publication Data

Your first 100 words in Persian : Persian for total beginners through puzzles and games / series concept, Jane Wightwick ; illustrations, Mahmoud Gaafar ; Persian edition, Abdi Rafiee.
       p.   cm.
   English and Persian.
   ISBN 0-07-141224-7
    1. Persian language—Textbooks for foreign speakers—English.   2. Persian language—Glossaries, vocabularies, etc.   I. Title: Your first one hundred words in Persian.   II. Wightwick, Jane.   III. Gaafar, Mahmoud.   IV. Rafiee, Abdi.

PK6239.5.E5Y68   2004
491′.5582421—dc22   2004052845

10 DIG/DIG 13

ISBN 0-07-141224-7

McGraw-Hill books are available at special quantity discounts to use as premiums and sales promotions, or for use in corporate training programs. For more information, please write to the Director of Special Sales, Professional Publishing, McGraw-Hill, Two Penn Plaza, New York, NY 10121-2298. Or contact your local bookstore.

Other titles in this series:

Your First 100 Words in Arabic
Your First 100 Words in Chinese
Your First 100 Words in French
Your First 100 Words in German
Your First 100 Words in Greek
Your First 100 Words in Hebrew
Your First 100 Words in Italian
Your First 100 Words in Japanese
Your First 100 Words in Korean
Your First 100 Words in Pashto
Your First 100 Words in Russian
Your First 100 Words in Spanish

This book is printed on acid-free paper.

◎ CONTENTS

⊚ INTRODUCTION

In this activity book you'll find 100 key words for you to learn to read in Persian. All the activities are designed specifically for reading non-Latin script languages. Many of the activities are inspired by the kind of games used to teach children to read their own language: flashcards, matching games, memory games, joining exercises, etc. This is not only a more effective method of learning to read a new script, but also much more fun.

We've included a **Scriptbreaker** to get you started. This is a friendly introduction to the Persian script that will give you tips on how to remember the letters.

Then you can move on to the eight **Topics**. Each topic presents essential words in large type. There is also a pronunciation guide so you know how to say the words. These words are also featured in the tear-out **Flashcard** section at the back of the book. When you've mastered the words, you can go on to try out the activities and games for that topic.

There's also a **Round-up** section to review all your new words and the **Answers** to all the activities to check yourself.

Follow this 4-step plan for maximum success:

1 Have a look at the key topic words with their pictures. Then tear out the flashcards and shuffle them. Put them Persian side up. Try to remember what the word means and turn the card over to check with the English. When you can do this, cover the pronunciation and try to say the word and remember the meaning by looking at the Persian script only.

2 Put the cards English side up and try to say the Persian word. Try the cards again each day both ways around. (When you can remember a card for seven days in a row, you can file it.)

3 Try out the activities and games for each topic. This will re-inforce your recognition of the key words.

4 After you have covered all the topics, you can try the activities in the **Round-up** section to test your knowledge of all the 100 words in the book. You can also try shuffling all the flashcards together to see how many you can remember.

This flexible and fun way of reading your first words in Persian should give you a head start whether you're learning at home or in a group.

The purpose of this Scriptbreaker is to introduce you to the Persian script and how it is formed. You should not try to memorize the alphabet at this stage, nor try to write the letters yourself. Instead, have a quick look through this section and then move on to the topics, glancing back if you want to work out the letters in a particular word. Remember, though, that recognizing the whole shape of the word in an unfamiliar script is just as important as knowing how it is made up. Using this method you will have a much more instinctive recall of vocabulary and will gain the confidence to expand your knowledge in other directions.

Persian is written in the Arabic script with some modified characters. Reading the script is not nearly as difficult as it might seem at first glance. There are 32 letters, no capital letters, and, unlike English, words are generally spelled as they sound. There are two main points to etch into your brain:

- Persian is written from right to left.
- The letters are "joined up" — you cannot "print" a word as you can in English.

◎ The alphabet

The easiest way of tackling the alphabet is to divide it into similarly shaped letters. For example, here are two groups of similar letters. The only difference between them is the dots:

ح (the letter *he-jeemee*)   ب (the letter *beh*)

ج (the letter *jeem*)   ت (the letter *teh*)

خ (the letter *kheh*)   ث (the letter *seh*)

چ (the letter *cheh*)   پ (the letter *peh*)

When these letters join to other letters they change their shape. The most common change is that they lose their "tails":

$$ تج = ج + ت \qquad حب = ب + ح \quad \text{(read from } right \text{ to } left\text{)} $$

Because letters change their shape like this, they have an *initial*, a *medial* (middle) and a *final* form. For example, the letter ج (*jeem*) changes like this:

at the beginning of a word (*initial*)   ...ج

in the middle of a word (*medial*)   ...ج...

at the end of a word (*final*)   ج...

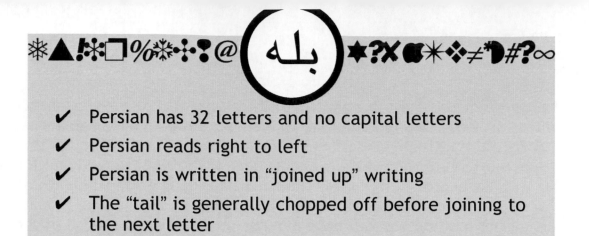

✔ Persian has 32 letters and no capital letters
✔ Persian reads right to left
✔ Persian is written in "joined up" writing
✔ The "tail" is generally chopped off before joining to the next letter

A few letters change their shapes completely depending on where they fall in a word. For example, the letter ه (*heh-do-chesm*) changes like this:

In addition, there are seven letters which *never* join to the letter *following* (to their left) and so hardly change shape at all. These are:

و (*vaav*)   ا (*alef*)

د (*daal*)   ذ (*zaal*)

ر (*reh*)   ز (*zeh*)   ژ (*zheh*)

You will find more details of how the individual letters change their shape in the table on page 8.

◎ Formation of words

We can use the principles of joining letters to form words.

So, for example, the Persian word for "hotel" is the same as English and written like this:

(hotel) هـتل = (l) ل + (t) ت + (h) ه ⟵

The Persian word for "sock" (*jooraab*), contains three non-joining letters and is written like this:

(jooraab) جوراب = (b) ب + (aa) ا + (r) ر + (oo) و + (j) ج ⟵

You may have noticed that some of the vowels seem to be missing from the script. In modern Persian, the short vowels (*a, e, o*) are not written as part of the script but as vowel signs above or below the letter. The short *a* is written as a dash above the letter (_ُ); the short *e* as a dash below (_ِ); and the short *o* as a comma-shape above (_ُ). This is similar to English shorthand, where we might write "bnk" instead of "bank." Here is "hotel" again, this time with the vowel signs:

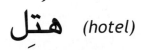 (hotel)

In this book we have included these vowel signs in the topics, but dropped them in the review section (*Round-up*). Most material for native speakers will leave them out as you are presumed to know them. This makes it all the more important for you to start recognizing a word without the short vowels.

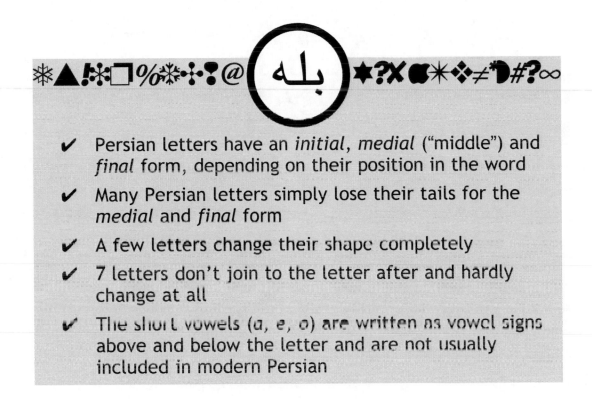

✔ Persian letters have an *initial*, *medial* ("middle") and *final* form, depending on their position in the word

✔ Many Persian letters simply lose their tails for the *medial* and *final* form

✔ A few letters change their shape completely

✔ 7 letters don't join to the letter after and hardly change at all

✔ The short vowels (*a*, *e*, *o*) are written as vowel signs above and below the letter and are not usually included in modern Persian

◎ Pronunciation tips

This activity book has simplified some aspects of pronunciation in order to emphasize the basics. Don't worry at this stage about being precisely correct — the other letters in a word will help you to be understood. Many Persian letters are pronounced in a similar way to their English equivalents, but here are a few that need special attention:

ق (*ghaaf*)/غ (*ghein*) both letters are pronounced like the French "r" as in "rue"

خ (*kheh*)　　　　　like the "ch" in the Yiddish "chutzpah" or the German "Bach"

ع (*ein*)　　　　　a glottal stop, similar to the sound made when "bottle" is pronounced with a London cockney accent — *bo'le*

If you look at the alphabet table below, you will notice that a single sound can be represented by two or more letters. For example, the sound t, can be written with the letter ت (teh) or with the letter ط (taa).

◎ Summary of the Persian alphabet

The table below shows all the Persian letters in the three positions, with the Persian letter name, followed by the sound. Remember that this is just for reference and you shouldn't expect to take it all in at once. If you know the basic principles of how the Persian script works, you will slowly come to recognize the individual letters.

	initial: medial: final:			initial: medial: final:			initial: medial: final:
alef *	ا ـا ا	reh r	ر ر ر	feh f	ف ـفـ ـف
beh b	ﺑ ـبـ ب	zeh z	ز ز ز	ghaaf gh	ﻗ ـقـ ق
peh p	ﭘ ـپـ پ	zheh zh	ژ ژ ژ	kaaf k	ﻛ ـكـ ک
teh t	ﺗ ـتـ ت	seen s	ﺳ ـسـ س	gaaf g	ﮔ ـگـ گ
seh s	ﺛ ـثـ ث	sheen sh	ﺷ ـشـ ش	laam l	ﻟ ـلـ ل
jeem j	ﺟ ـجـ ج	saad s	ﺻ ـصـ ص	meem m	ﻣ ـمـ م
cheh ch	ﭼ ـچـ چ	zaad z	ﺿ ـضـ ض	noon n	ﻧ ـنـ ن
heh-jeemee h	ﺣ ـحـ ح	taa t	ﻃ ﻃ ط	vaav v/oo/o	و و و
kheh kh	ﺧ ـخـ خ	zaa z	ﻇ ﻇ ظ	heh-do-chesm h	ﻫ ـهـ ـه/ه
daal d	د د د	ein '	ﻋ ـعـ ـع/ع	yeh y/ee	ﻳ ـيـ ی
zaal z	ذ ذ ذ	ghein gh	ﻏ ـغـ ـغ/غ		

* Any vowel in initial position and also aa in medial and final positions.

Note the special combination when alef is written after laam: ﻻ, as in ﺣﻻ (haalaa, meaning "now").

8

❶ AROUND THE HOME

Look at the pictures of things you might find in a house.
Tear out the flashcards for this topic.
Follow steps 1 and 2 of the plan in the introduction.

میز
meez

تِلویزیون
televeezyon

پَنجَره
panjareh

صَندَلی
sandalee

کامپیوتِر
kuumpyooter

تِلِفُن
telefon

کاناپِه
kaanaapeh

تَختِ خواب
takhteh khaab

یَخچال
yakhchaal

قَفَسه
ghafaseh

خوراکپَز
khoraakpaz

دَر
dar

Match the pictures with the words, as in the example.

كاناپه

تَختِ خواب

پَنجَره

میز

تِلِویزیون

صَندَلی

کامپیوتِر

تِلِفُن

Now match the Persian household words to the English.

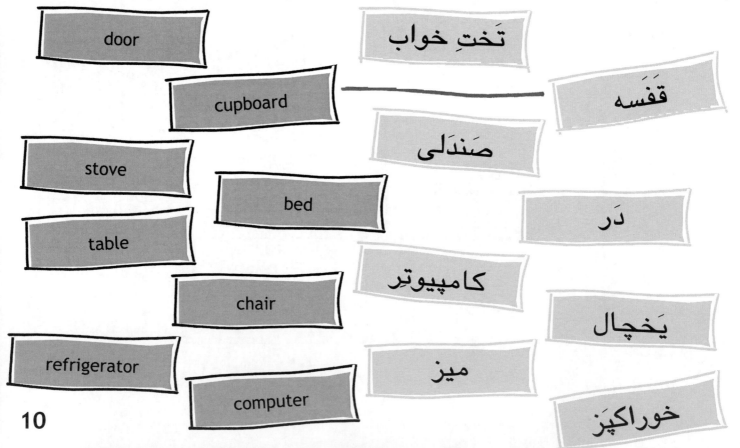

English	Persian
door	تَختِ خواب
cupboard	قَفَسه
stove	صَندَلی
bed	دَر
table	کامپیوتِر
chair	یَخچال
refrigerator	میز
computer	خوراکپَز

10

Match the words and their pronunciation.

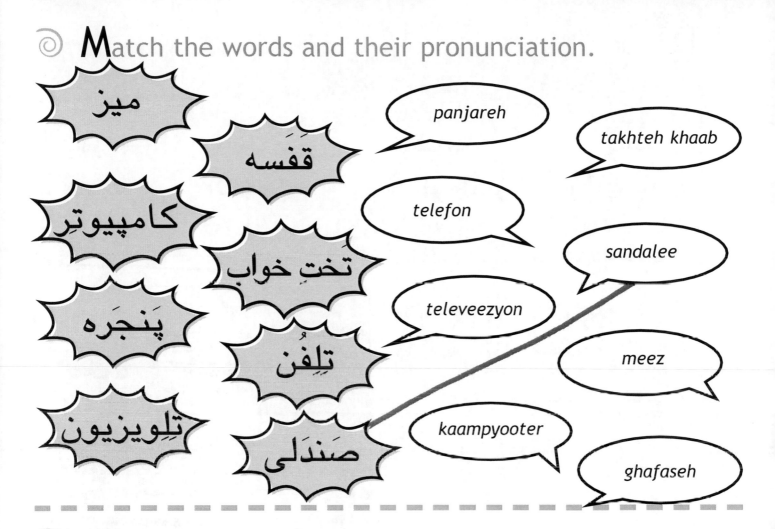

See if you can find these words in the word square.
The words run *right to left*.

يَخچال
ميز
صَندَلی
دَر
كاناپه
قَفَسه

ف	و	ه‍ پ	ا ن	ن ا	ا ك
ط	ی ل	د ن	ص ا	ف
د	ه‍ت ز	ل چ ر	د
ه‍ ب	ه‍ س ف ق و	ظ
ر	ف ی لا	ا ك ن	ص
ن	ي ا ج	س پ	ع ط
ل	ا خ چ ي	ذ	ف و
ث	ز م‍ي ح	پ ا	ب

Decide where the household items should go. Then write the correct number in the picture, as in the example.

10 کامپیوتِر	7 قَفَسه	4 تِلویزیون	1 میز
11 پَنجَره	8 خوراکپَز	5 تِلِفُن	2 صَندَلی
12 دَر	9 یَخچال	6 تَختِ خواب	3 کاناپه

12

Now see if you can fill in the household word at the bottom of the page by choosing the correct Persian.

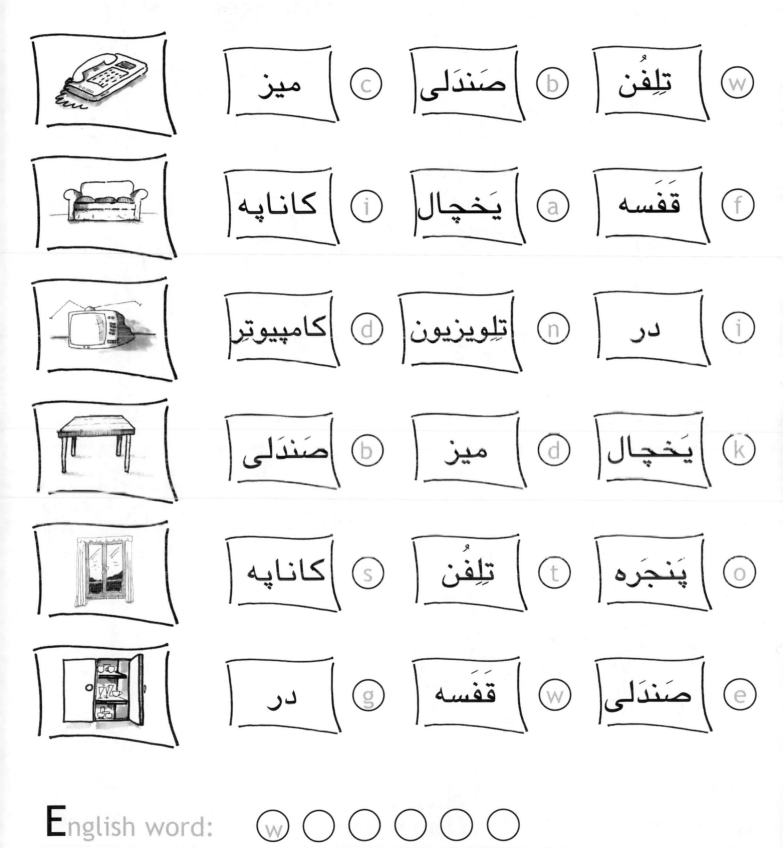

w تِلِفُن	b صَندَلی	c میز
f قَفَسه	a یَخچال	i کاناپه
i در	n تِلِویزیون	d کامپیوتِر
k یَخچال	d میز	b صَندَلی
o پَنجَره	t تِلِفُن	s کاناپه
e صَندَلی	w قَفَسه	g در

English word: (w) ( ) ( ) ( ) ( ) ( )

13

❷ CLOTHES

Look at the pictures of different clothes.
Tear out the flashcards for this topic.
Follow steps 1 and 2 of the plan in the introduction.

كَمَربَند
kamarband

پوليور
poleever

شورت
short

شَلوار
shalvaar

جوراب
jooraab

تى شِرت
tee shert

دامَن *daaman*

پالتو
paalto

كُلاه
kolaah

پيراهَنِ زنانه
peeraahaneh zanaaneh

كَفش *kafsh*

پيراهَنِ مَردانه
peeraahaneh mardaaneh

Match the Persian words and their pronunciation.

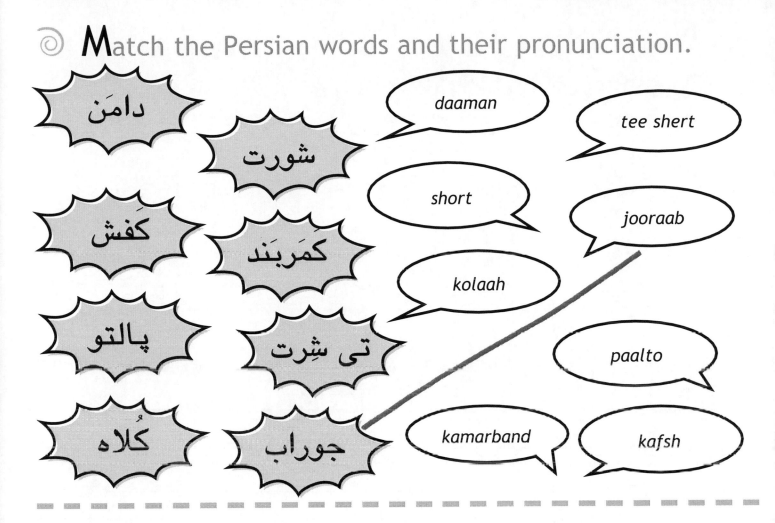

دامَن

شورت

کَفش

کَمَربَند

پالتو

تی شِرت

کُلاه

جوراب

daaman

tee shert

short

jooraab

kolaah

paalto

kamarband

kafsh

See if you can find these clothes in the word square.

The words run *right to left*.

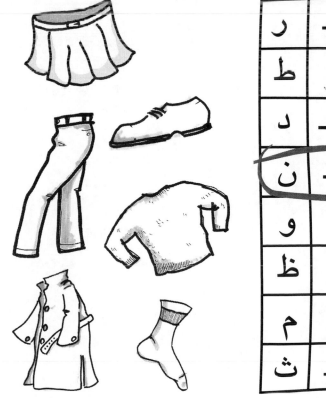

ق	ي	ث	ب	ل	پ	ف	ر
ك	ق	ش	ل	و	ا	ر	ط
ج	و	ر	ا	ب	ت	ه	د
ظ	و	ق	ف	د	ا	م	ن
م	ي	چ	پ	ا	ل	ت	و
ف	ن	ك	ف	ش	ن	ي	ظ
و	پ	و	ل	ي	و	ر	م
ح	ذ	ا	چ	غ	پ	ف	ث

15

Now match the Persian words, their pronunciation, and the English meaning, as in the example.

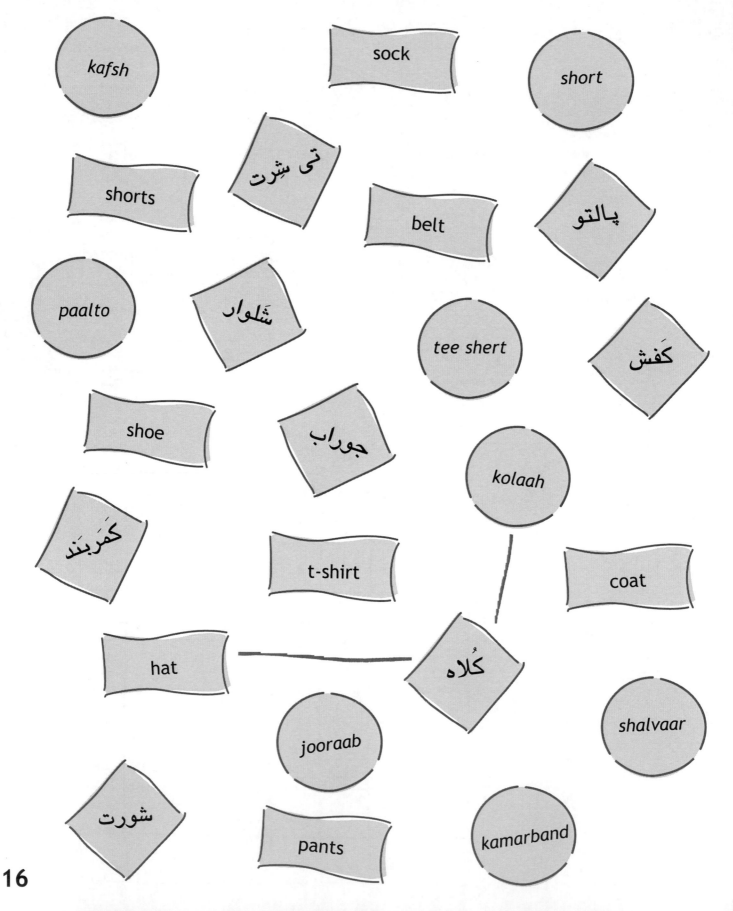

kafsh

sock

short

تی شِرت

shorts

belt

پالتو

paalto

شَلوار

tee shert

کَفش

shoe

جوراب

kolaah

کَمَربَند

t-shirt

coat

hat

کُلاه

shalvaar

jooraab

شورت

pants

kamarband

Candy is going on vacation. Count how many of each type of clothing she is packing in her suitcase.

كُلاه	2	پالتو	☐	كَمَربَند	☐	كَفش	☐
شَلوار	☐	شورت	☐	پيراهَنِ زَنانه	☐	جوراب	☐
دامَن	☐	تى شِرت	☐	پيراهَنِ مَردانه	☐	پوليوِر	☐

Someone has ripped up the Persian words for clothes.
Can you join the two halves of the words, as the example?

❸ AROUND TOWN

Look at the pictures of things you might find around town.
Tear out the flashcards for this topic.
Follow steps 1 and 2 of the plan in the introduction.

هُتِل
hotel

اُتوبوس
otoboos

خانه
khaaneh

دوچَرخه
docharkheh

ماشین
maasheen

سینما seenemaa

قَطار ghataar

تاکسی taaksee

مَدرِسه madreseh

جاده jaaddeh

فُروشگاه
forooshgaah

رِستوران
restooraan

◎ **M**atch the Persian words to their English equivalents.

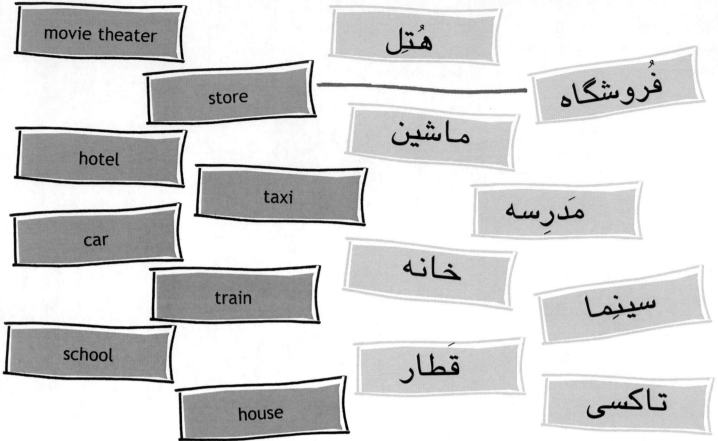

movie theater

store

hotel

taxi

car

train

school

house

هُتِل

فُروشگاه

ماشین

مَدرِسه

خانه

سینِما

قَطار

تاکسی

◎ **N**ow list the correct order of the English words to match the Persian word chain, as in the example.

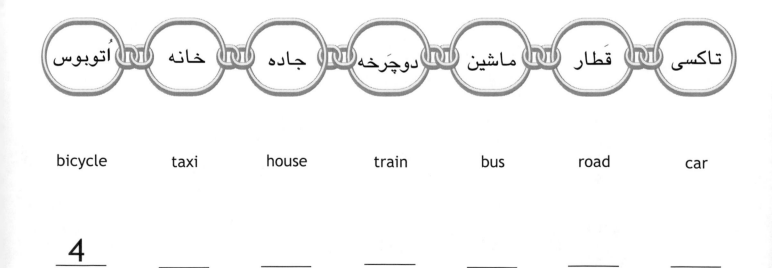

اُتوبوس — خانه — جاده — دوچَرخه — ماشین — قَطار — تاکسی

bicycle   taxi   house   train   bus   road   car

4 ___ ___ ___ ___ ___ ___

20

 **M**atch the words to the signs.

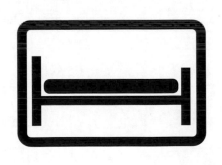 

اُتوبوس	دوچَرخه	ماشین	مَدرِسه
تاکسی	هُتِل	قَطار	رِستوران

21

Now choose the Persian word that matches the picture to fill in the English word at the bottom of the page.

Now match the Persian to the pronunciation.

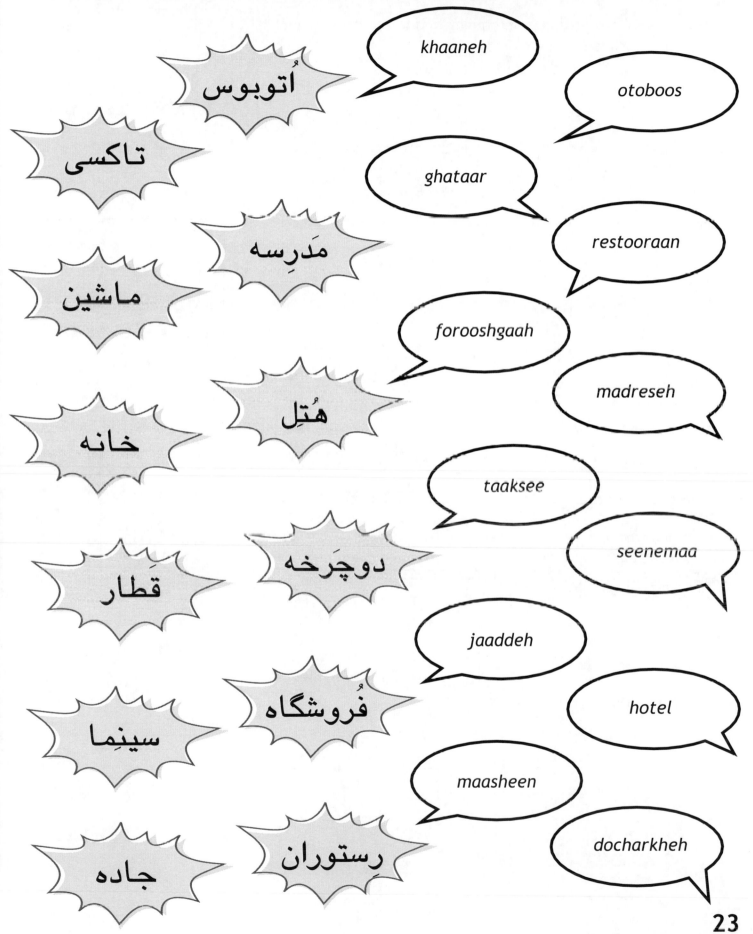

4 COUNTRYSIDE

Look at the pictures of things you might find in the countryside.
Tear out the flashcards for this topic.
Follow steps 1 and 2 of the plan in the introduction.

تپه _tappeh_

کوه _kooh_

پُل _pol_

مَزرَعه _mazra'eh_

دَریاچه _daryaacheh_

دِرَخت _derakht_

گل _gol_

رود _rood_

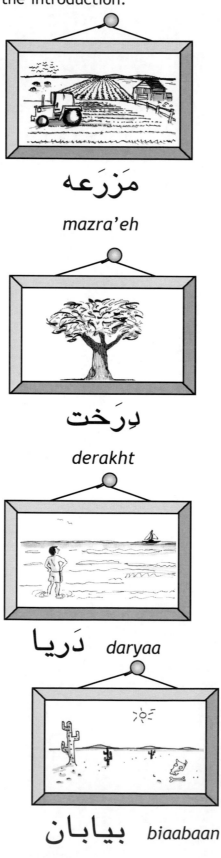

دَریا _daryaa_

کِشتزار _keshtzaar_

بیابان _biaabaan_

جَنگل _jangal_

Can you match all the countryside words to the pictures?

كوه

مَزرَعه

دَريا

جَنگل

بيابان

تَپه

دَرياچه

پُل

رود

گل

دِرَخت

كِشتزار

25

Now check (✔) the features you can find in this landscape.

پُل ✔		دِرَخت ☐		بیابان ☐		تَپه ☐
کوه ☐		دَریا ☐		کِشتزار ☐		جَنگل ☐
دَریاچه ☐		رود ☐		گل ☐		مَزرَعه ☐

◎ **M**atch the Persian words and their pronunciation.

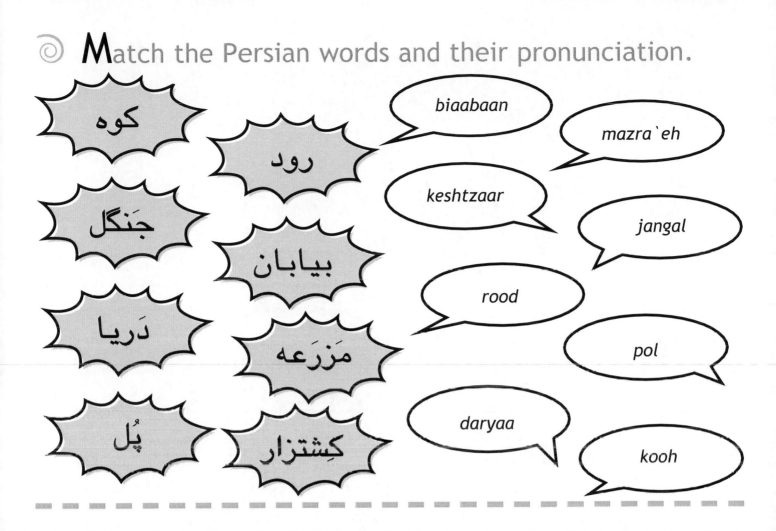

- -

◎ **S**ee if you can find these words in the word square.

The words run *right to left*.

درخت

مزرعه

تپه

گل

پل

دریاچه

د	ر	ا	چ	پ	ل	و	ک
ف	ا	ص	ت	پ	ه	ی	ط
د	ر	چ	ل	ز	ت	ه	د
گ	و	د	ر	ت	خ	ب	ه
ص	ن	ک	ا	لا	ی	ف	ک
ط	د	ر	ی	ا	چ	ه	پ
و	ف	ذ	ی	خ	چ	گ	ل
ب	م	ز	ر	ع	ه	ز	ف

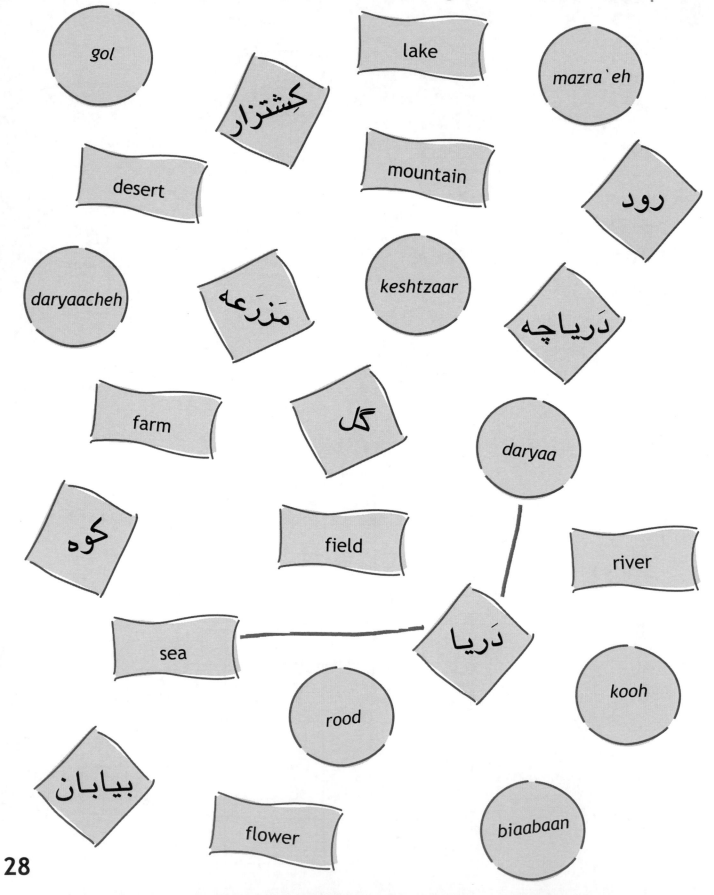

Finally, test yourself by joining the Persian words, their pronunciation, and the English meanings, as in the example.

gol

lake

mazra`eh

کشتزار

desert

mountain

رود

daryaacheh

مَزرعه

keshtzaar

دَریاچه

farm

گل

daryaa

کوه

field

river

sea

دَریا

kooh

rood

بیابان

flower

biaabaan

28

⑤ OPPOSITES

Look at the pictures.
Tear out the flashcards for this topic.
Follow steps 1 and 2 of the plan in the introduction.

كَثيف
kaseef

تَميز
tameez

كوچِک
koochek

بُزُرگ
bozorg

اَرزان *arzaan*

سبُک *sabok*

آهِستہ *aahesteh*

گِران *geraan*

سَنگين *sangeen*

تُند *tond*

قَديمی *ghadeemee*

جَديد *jadeed*

29

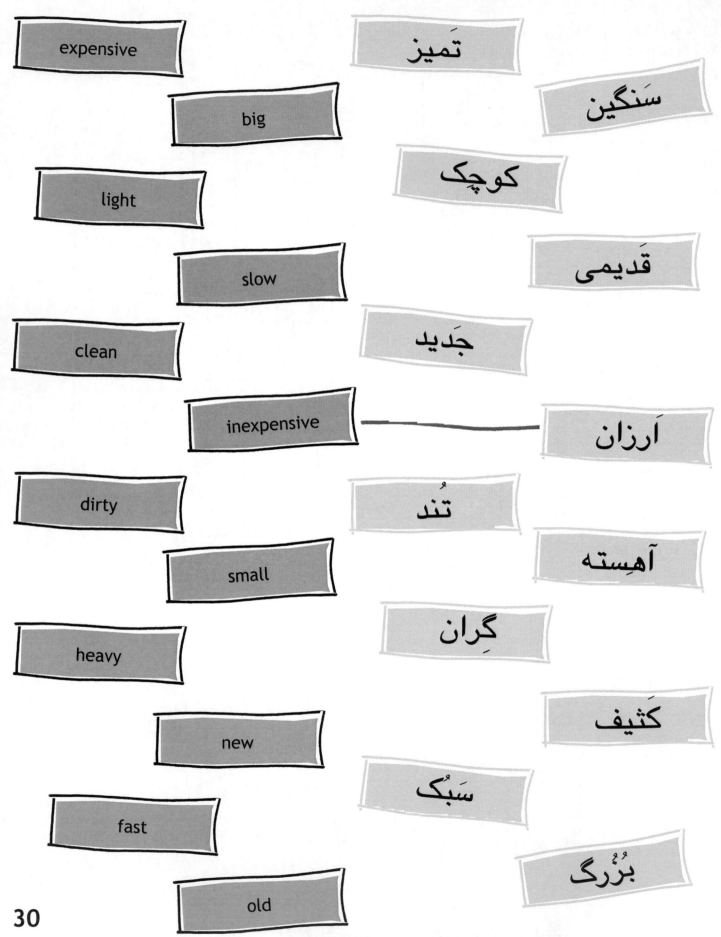

expensive

تَمیز

big

سَنگین

light

کوچِک

slow

قَدیمی

clean

جَدید

inexpensive ———————————— اَرزان

dirty

تُند

small

آهِسته

heavy

گِران

new

کَثیف

fast

سَبُک

بُزُرگ

old

Now choose the Persian word that matches the picture to fill in the English word at the bottom of the page.

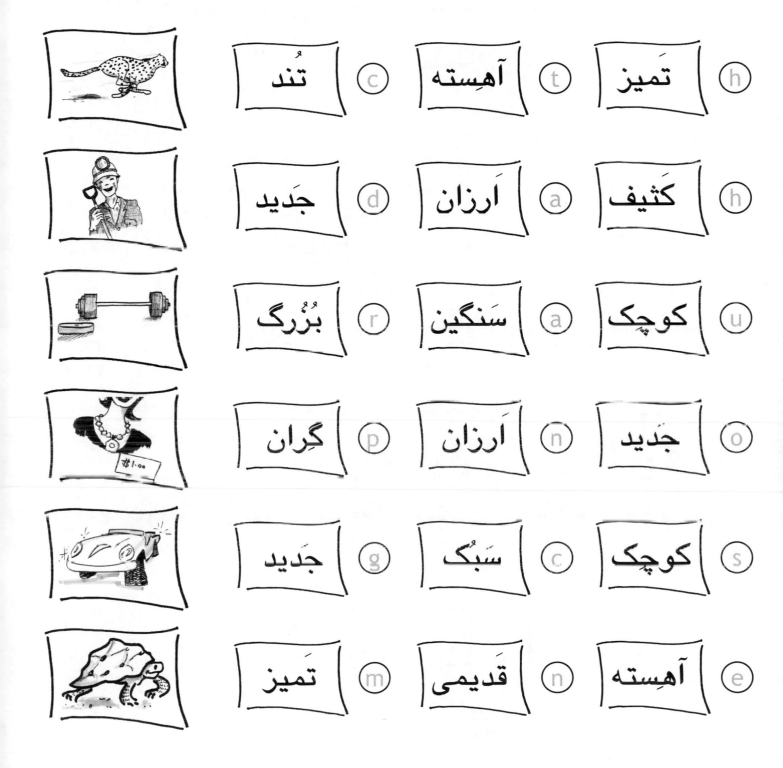

English word: ◯ ◯ ◯ ◯ ◯ ◯

Find the odd one out in these groups of words.

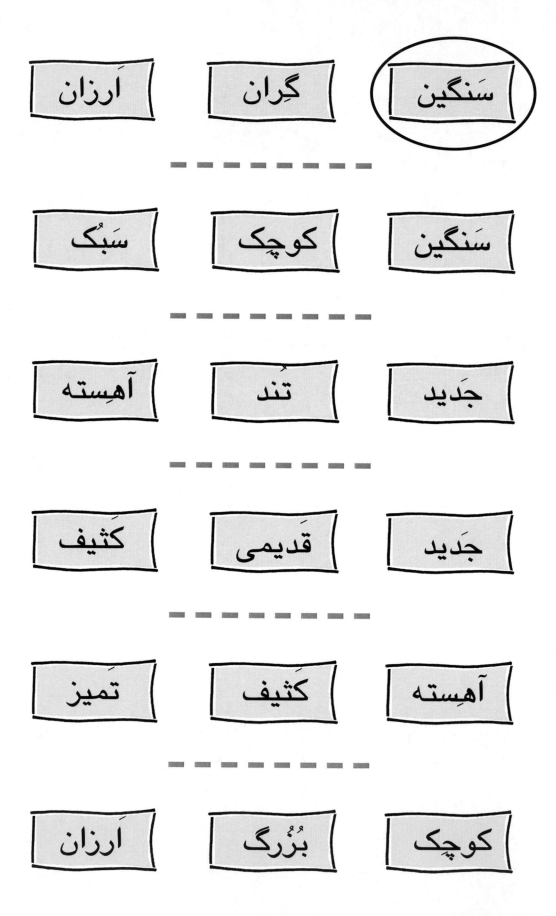

◎ **F**inally, join the English words to their Persian opposites, as in the example.

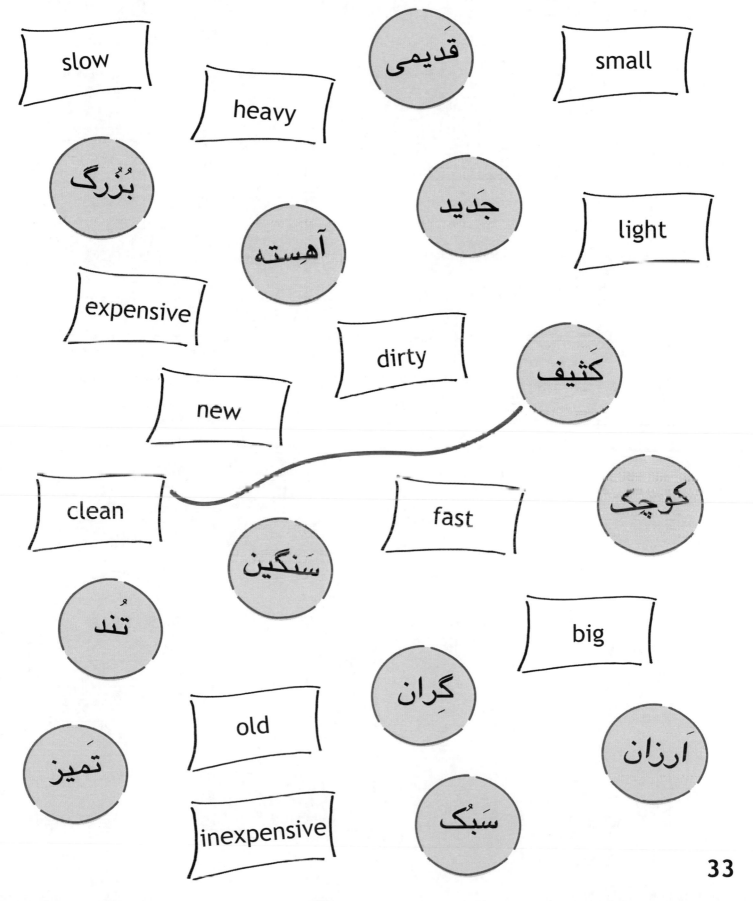

slow

قَدیمی

small

heavy

بُزُرگ

جَدید

light

آهِسته

expensive

dirty

كَثیف

new

كوچِك

clean

fast

سَنگین

تُند

big

گِران

اَرزان

old

تَمیز

inexpensive

سَبُک

33

6 ANIMALS

Look at the pictures.
Tear out the flashcards for this topic.
Follow steps 1 and 2 of the plan in the introduction.

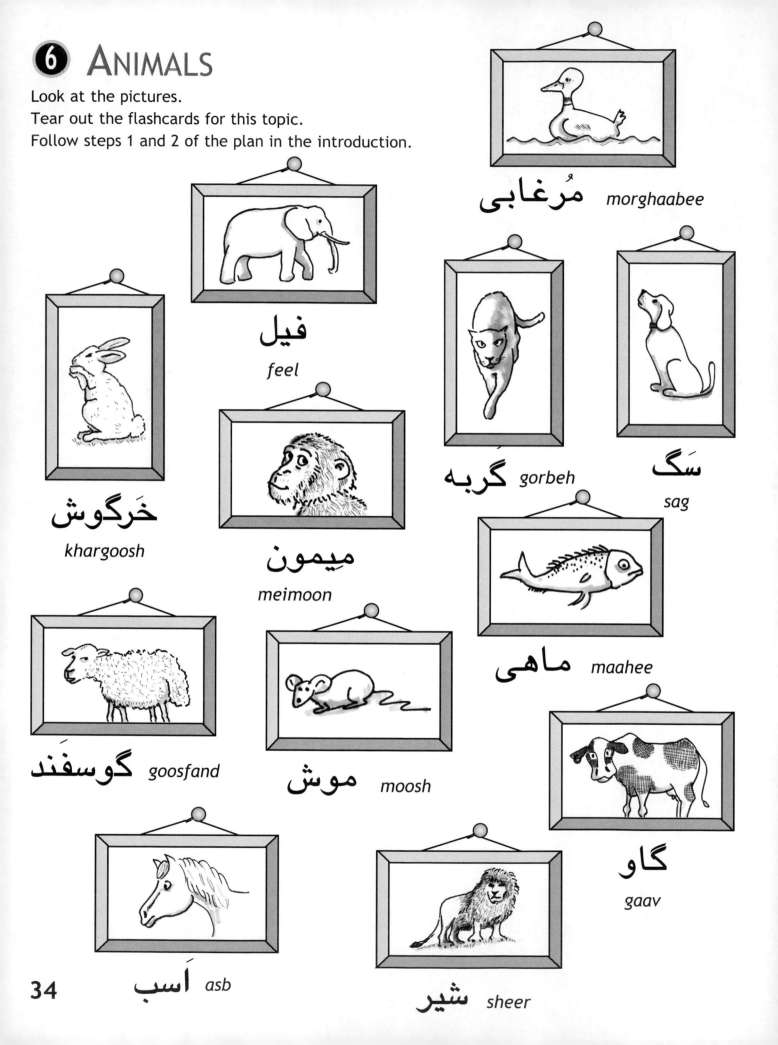

مُرغابی *morghaabee*

فیل *feel*

گربه *gorbeh*

سَگ *sag*

خَرگوش *khargoosh*

میمون *meimoon*

ماهی *maahee*

گوسفَند *goosfand*

موش *moosh*

گاو *gaav*

اَسب *asb*

شیر *sheer*

Match the animals to their associated pictures, as in the example.

خَرگوش

اَسب

میمون

گُربه

گوسفَند

موش

سَگ

شیر

ماهی

گاو

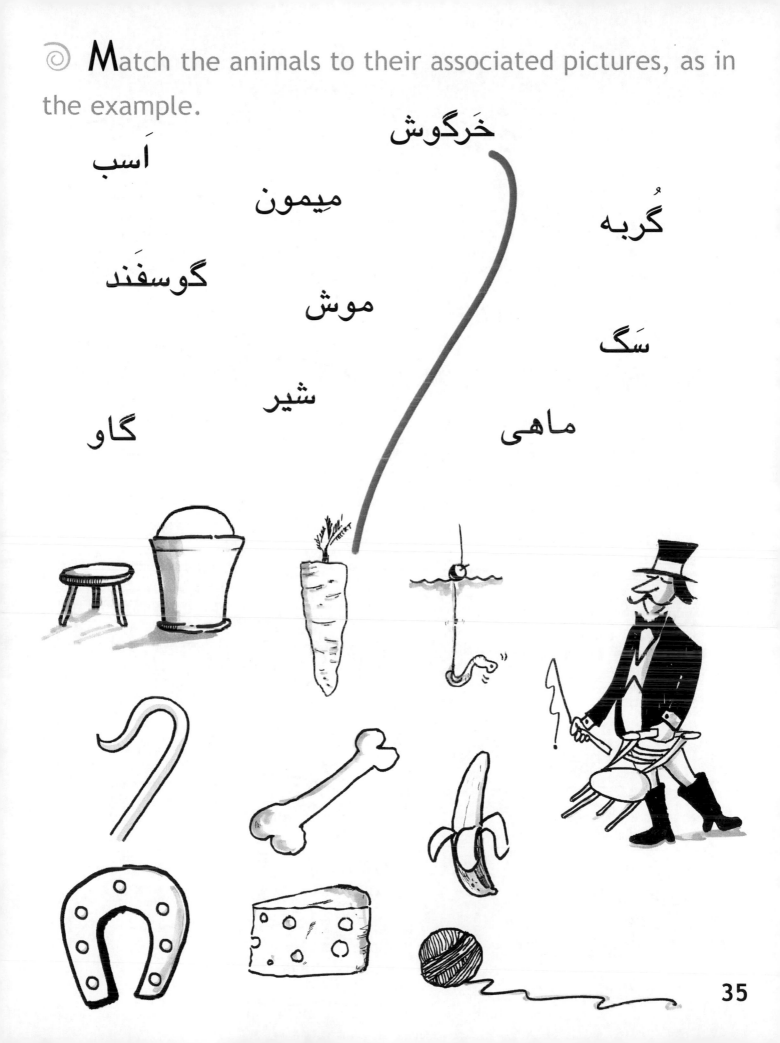

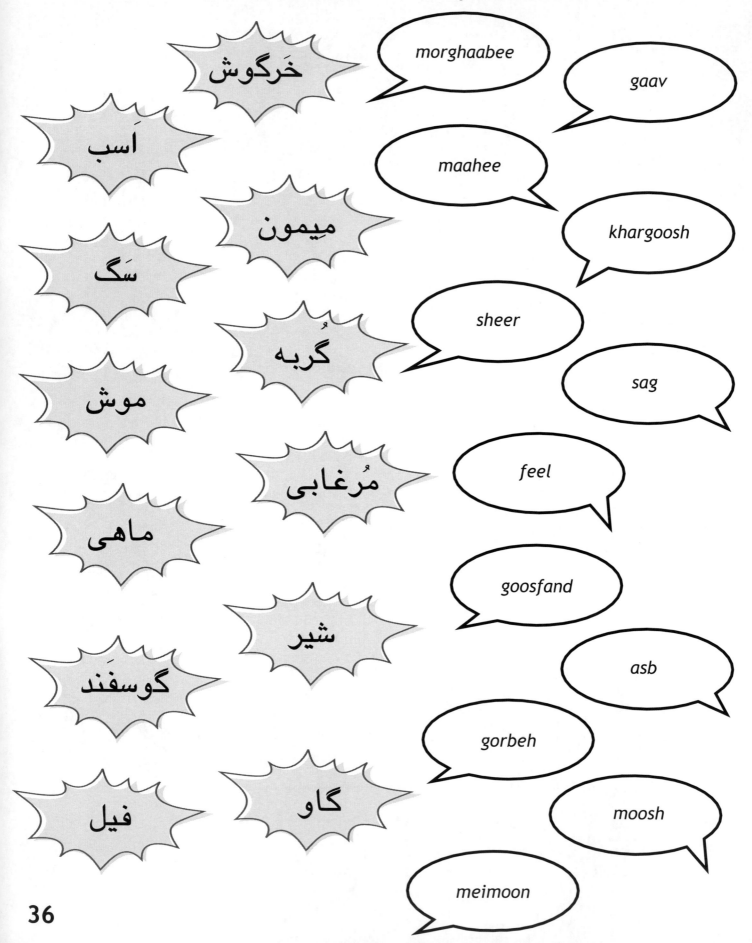

Check (✔) the animal words you can find in the word pile.

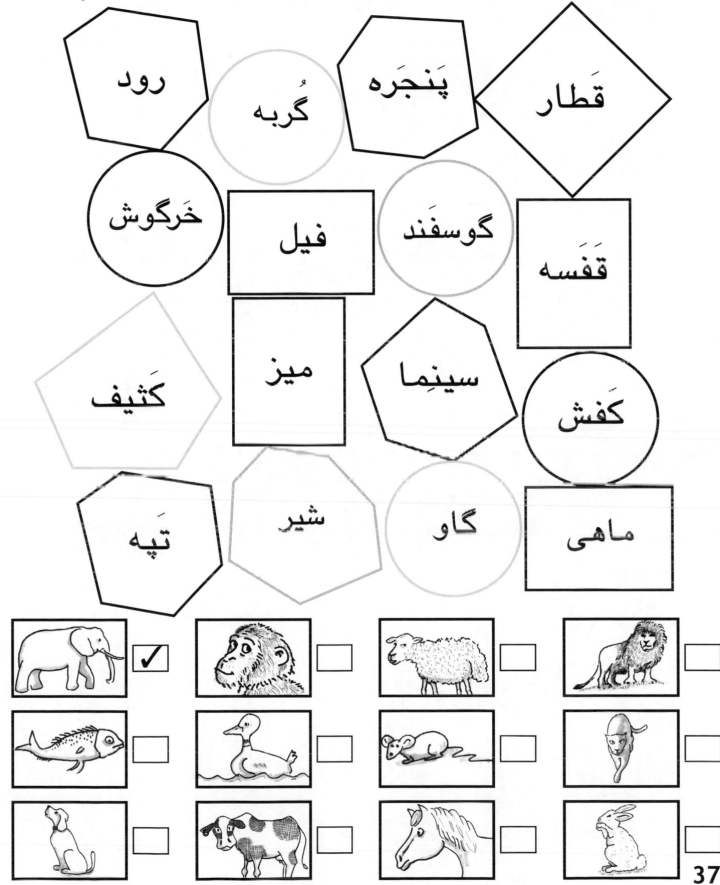

رود   گُربه   پَنجَره   قَطار

خَرگوش   فیل   گوسفَند   قَفَسه

کَثیف   میز   سینِما   کَفش

تَپه   شیر   گاو   ماهی

Join the Persian animals to their English equivalents.

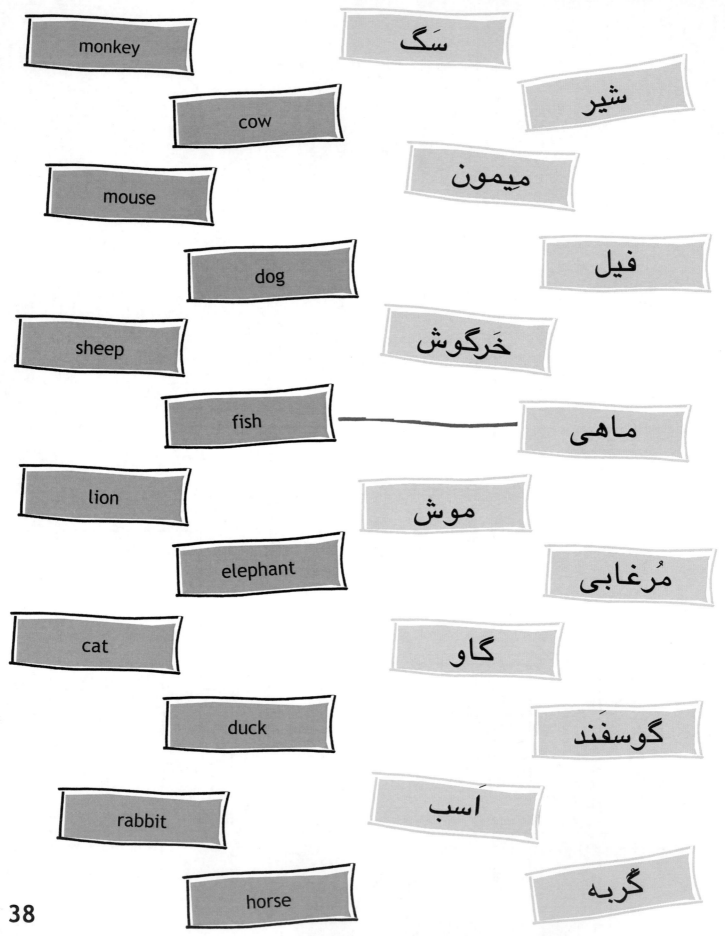

monkey

سَگ

شیر

cow

میمون

mouse

فیل

dog

خَرگوش

sheep

fish ——————— ماهی

lion

موش

elephant

مُرغابی

cat

گاو

duck

گوسفَند

اَسب

rabbit

گُربه

horse

38

❼ PARTS OF THE BODY

Look at the pictures of parts of the body.
Tear out the flashcards for this topic.
Follow steps 1 and 2 of the plan in the introduction.

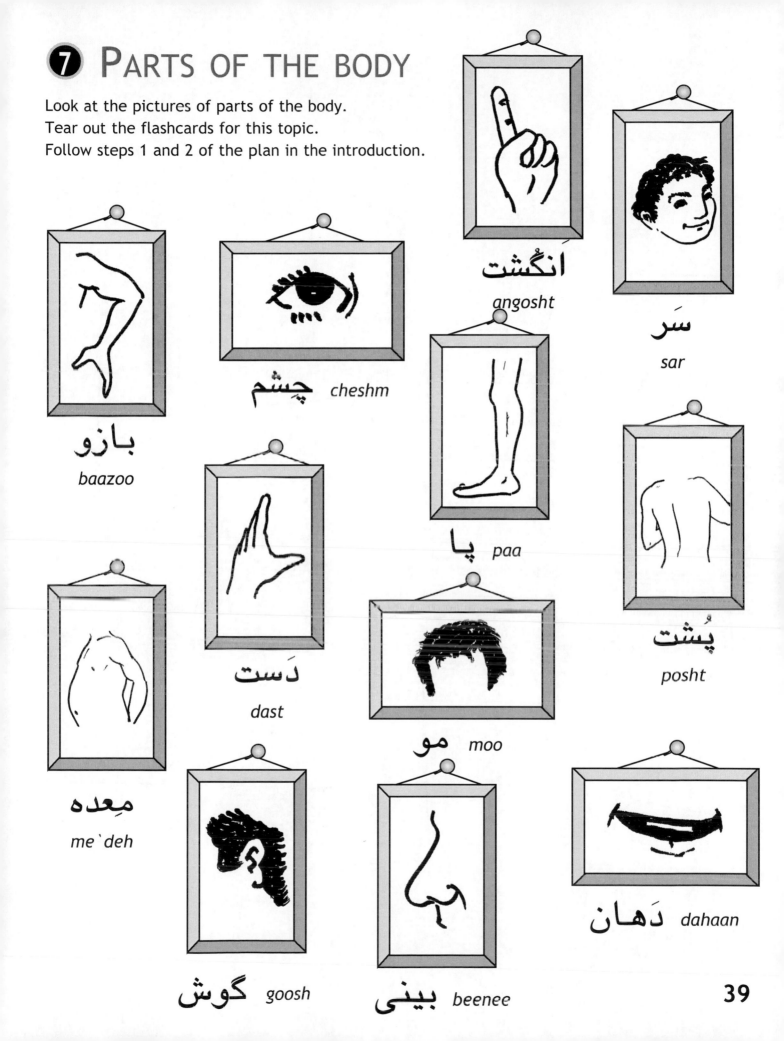

اَنگُشت
angosht

سَر
sar

بازو
baazoo

چِشم
cheshm

پا *paa*

پُشت
posht

دَست
dast

مو *moo*

مِعده
me`deh

گوش *goosh*

بینی *beenee*

دَهان *dahaan*

39

Someone has ripped up the Persian words for parts of the body. Can you join the two halves of the word again?

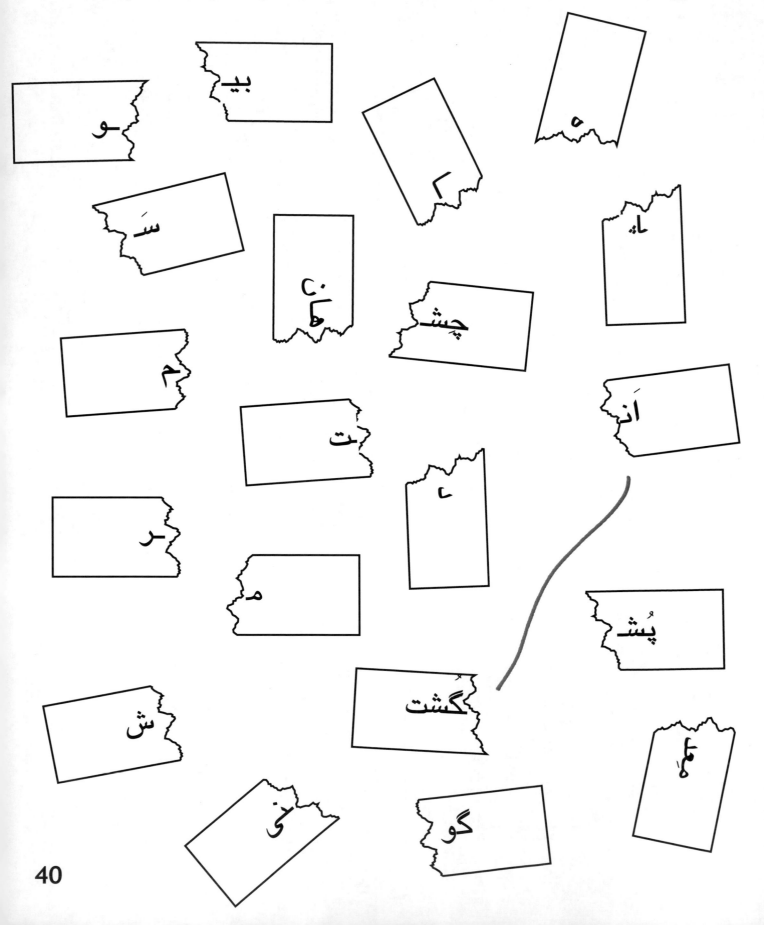

See if you can find and circle six parts of the body in the word square, then draw them in the boxes below.

The words run *right to left*.

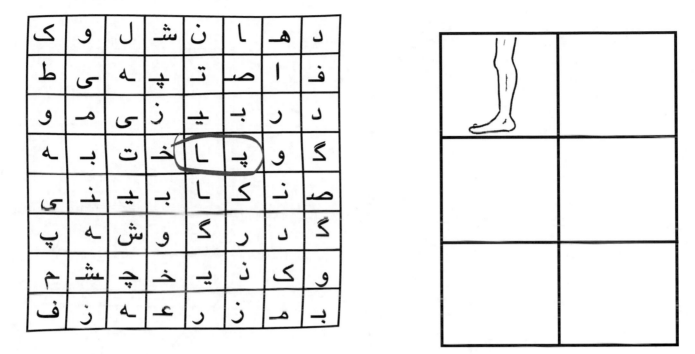

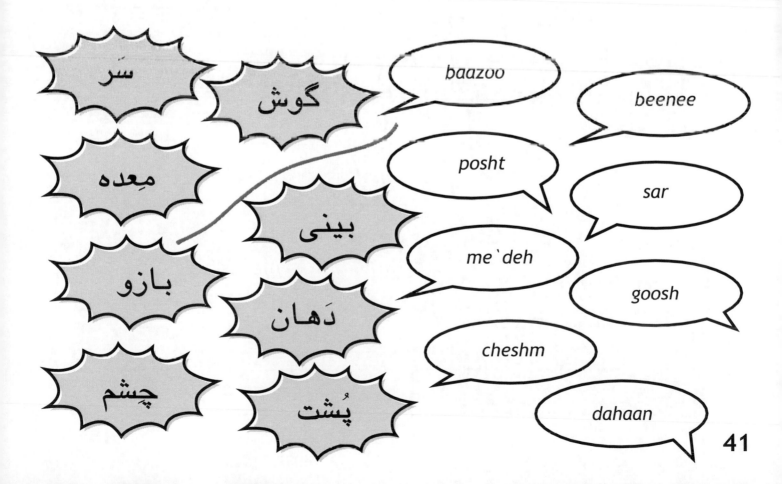

Label the body with the correct number, and write the pronunciation next to the words.

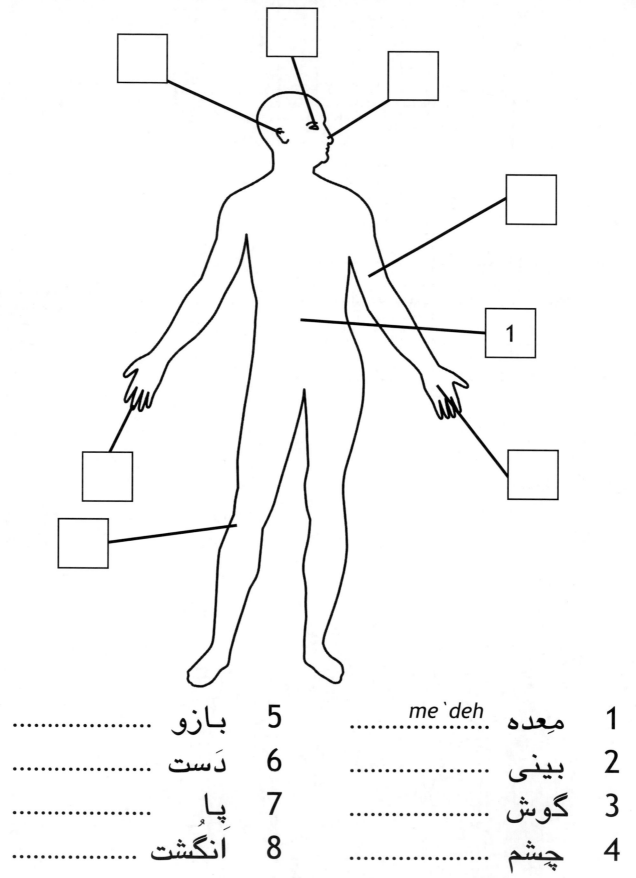

....	بازو	5	*me`deh*	مِعده	1
....	دَست	6	....	بینی	2
....	پاٰ	7	....	گوش	3
....	اَنگشت	8	....	چِشم	4

Finally, match the Persian words, their pronunciation, and the English meanings, as in the example.

angosht

hair

paa

پُشت

stomach

hand

بازو

baazoo

مو

dast

مِعده

back

انگُشت

goush

دَست

finger

arm

ear

گوش

posht

moo

پا

me'deh

leg

8 USEFUL EXPRESSIONS

Look at the pictures.
Tear out the flashcards for this topic.
Follow steps 1 and 2 of the plan in the introduction.

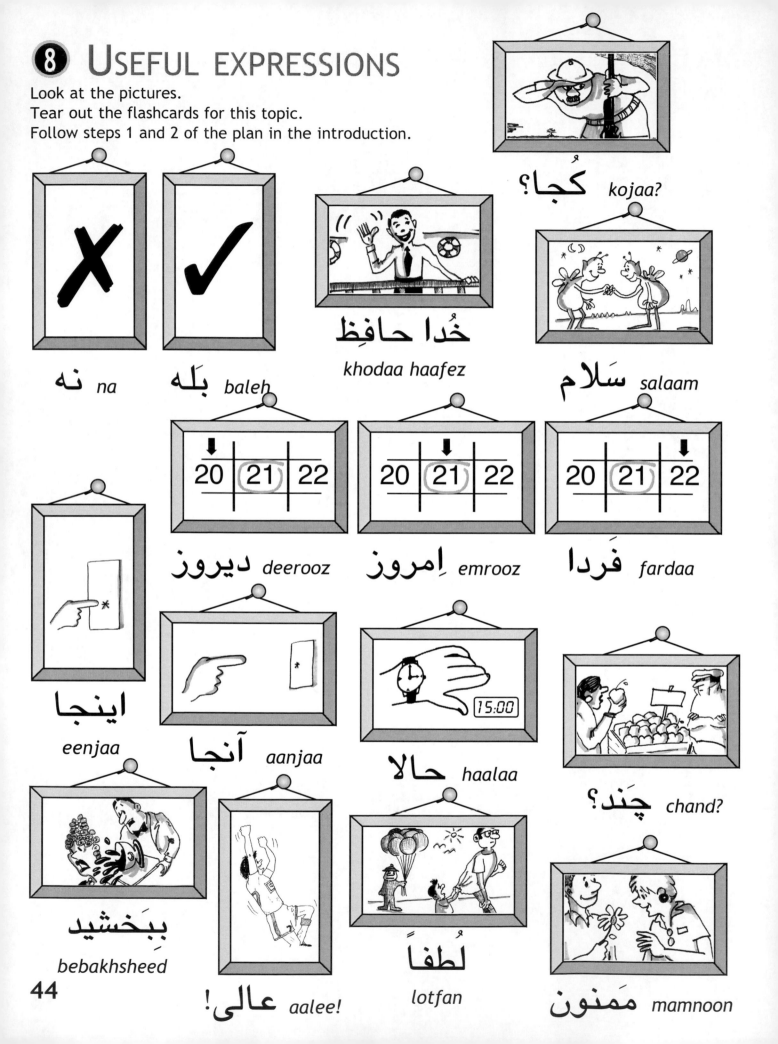

کُجا؟ *kojaa?*

خُدا حافِظ *khodaa haafez*

سَلام *salaam*

نه *na*

بَله *baleh*

دیروز *deerooz*

اِمروز *emrooz*

فَردا *fardaa*

اینجا *eenjaa*

آنجا *aanjaa*

حالا *haalaa*

چَند؟ *chand?*

بِبَخشید *bebakhsheed*

عالی! *aalee!*

لُطفاً *lotfan*

مَمنون *mamnoon*

44

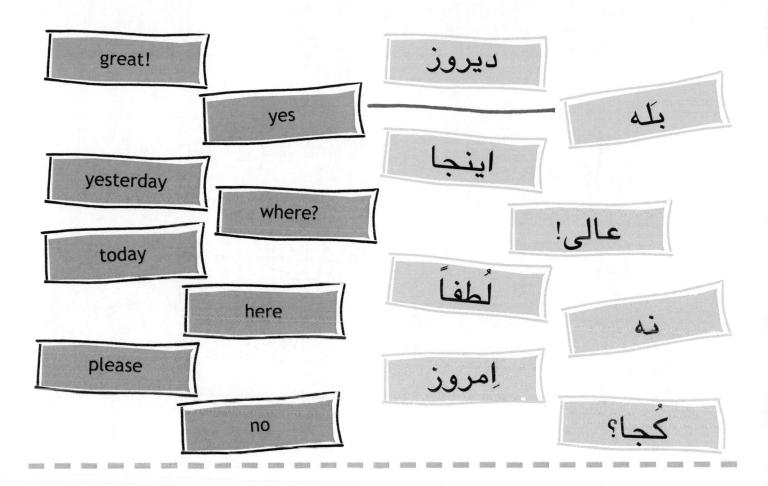

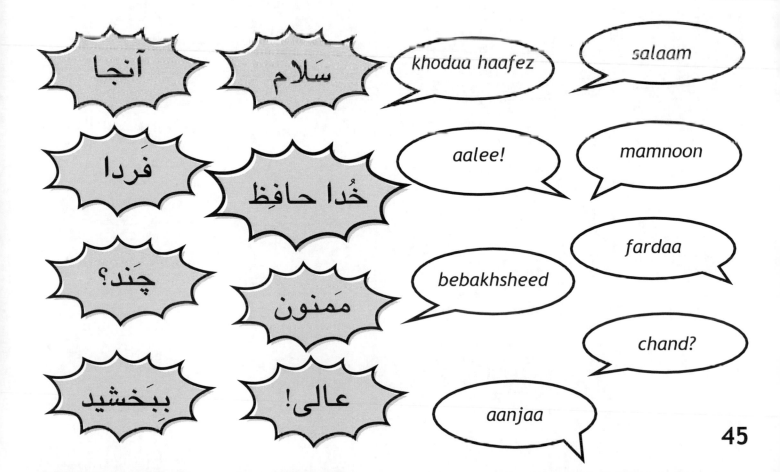

45

Choose the Persian word that matches the picture to fill in the English word at the bottom of the page.

اینجا (p)	نه (c)	بَله (t)
مَمنون (j)	حالا (a)	لُطفاً (l)
بَله (m)	نه (e)	اِمروز (i)
آنجا (b)	سَلام (a)	حالا (x)
کُجا؟ (s)	عالی! (h)	چَند؟ (t)
دیروز (b)	نه (y)	بَله (e)

English word: (p) ( ) ( ) ( ) ( ) ( )

What are these people saying? Write the correct number in each speech bubble, as in the example.

7 كُجا؟	5 اينجا	3 بَله	1 سَلام
8 چَند؟	6 بِبَخشيد	4 نه	2 لُطفاً

Finally, match the Persian words, their pronunciation, and the English meanings, as in the example.

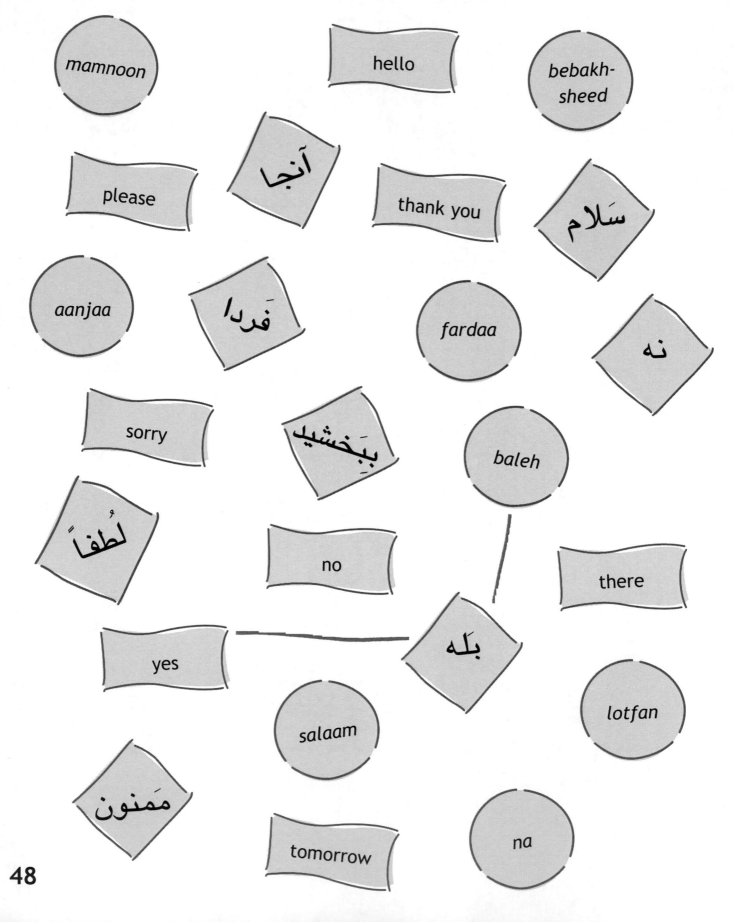

mamnoon

hello

bebakh-sheed

please

آنجا

thank you

سَلام

aanjaa

فَردا

fardaa

نه

sorry

بِبَخشيد

baleh

لُطفاً

no

there

yes

بَله

lotfan

salaam

na

مَمنون

tomorrow

● ROUND-UP

This section is designed to review all the 100 words you have met in the different topics. It is a good idea to test yourself with your flashcards before trying this section.

◎ These ten objects are hidden in the picture. Can you find and circle them?

صندلی   در   کلاه   دوچرخه   ماهی

سگ   تخت خواب   جوراب   پالتو   گل

49

See if you can remember all these words.

امروز

اتوبوس

تند

بینی

بیابان

بله

قفسه

شیر

پیراهن زنانه

ارزان

رود

پا

Find the odd one out in these groups of words and say why.

سگ	گاو	(میز)	میمون

Because it isn't an animal.

ماشین	اتوبوس	قطار	تلفن
کشتزار	پالتو	شورت	دامن
دریا	دریاچه	رود	درخت
سنگین	کثیف	تمیز	سینما
خرگوش	گربه	ماهی	شیر
بازو	کاناپه	سر	معده
لطفاً	دیروز	امروز	فردا
خوراکپز	تخت خواب	قفسه	یخچال

◎ **L**ook at the objects below for 30 seconds.

◎ **C**over the picture and try to remember all the objects.
Circle the Persian words for those you remember.

گل   کفش   ممنون   در

ماشین   نه   اینجا   پالتو   قطار

کمربند   کوه   اسب   صندلی

تخت خواب   چشم   تی شرت   جوراب

میمون   تلویزیون   تاکسی   شورت

Now match the Persian words, their pronunciation, and the English meanings, as in the example.

mamnoon

خانه

lake

khaaneh

bed

thank you

کجا؟

sangeen

جنگل

kojaa?

سنگین

where?

دریاچه

poleever

تخت خواب

house

forest

sweater

پولیور

daryaacheh

takhteh khaab

ممنون

heavy

jangal

Fill in the English phrase at the bottom of the page.

(w) كاناپه	(g) تاكسی	(t) بینی
(o) پالتو	(a) كثیف	(e) پل
(m) كجا؟	(l) چند؟	(i) اینجا
(b) گاو	(l) پنجره	(h) رستوران
(e) اسب	(a) چشم	(d) سگ
(o) چشم	(p) میز	(v) بله
(n) تپه	(y) نه	(r) در
(n) خرگوش	(e) جاده	(s) خوراكپز

English phrase: (w) ◯ ◯ ◯   ◯ ◯ ◯ ◯ !

Look at the two pictures and check (✔) the objects that are different in Picture B.

Picture A

Picture B

شورت ☐

تی شرت ☐

در ☐

گربه ☐

صندلی ☐

ماهی ☐

جوراب ☐

سگ ☐

55

◎ **N**ow join the Persian words to their English equivalents.

refrigerator

بازو

pants

معده

store

کوچک

school

یخچال

river

فروشگاه

great!

عالی!

small

رود

light

شلوار

arm

تمیز

stomach

سبک

clean

اسب

horse

مدرسه

Try to match the Persian to the pronunciation.

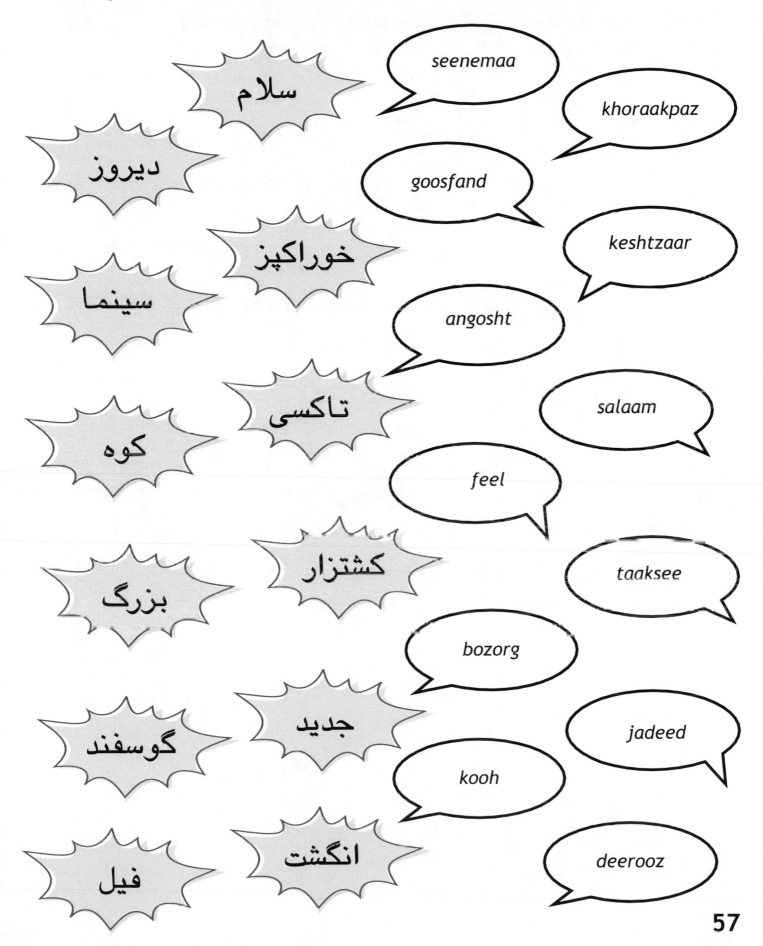

◎ Snake game.

● You will need a die and counter(s). You can challenge yourself to reach the finish or play with someone else. You have to throw the exact number to finish.

● Throw the die and move forward that number of spaces. When you land on a word you must pronounce it and say what it means in English. If you can't, you have to go back to the square you came from.

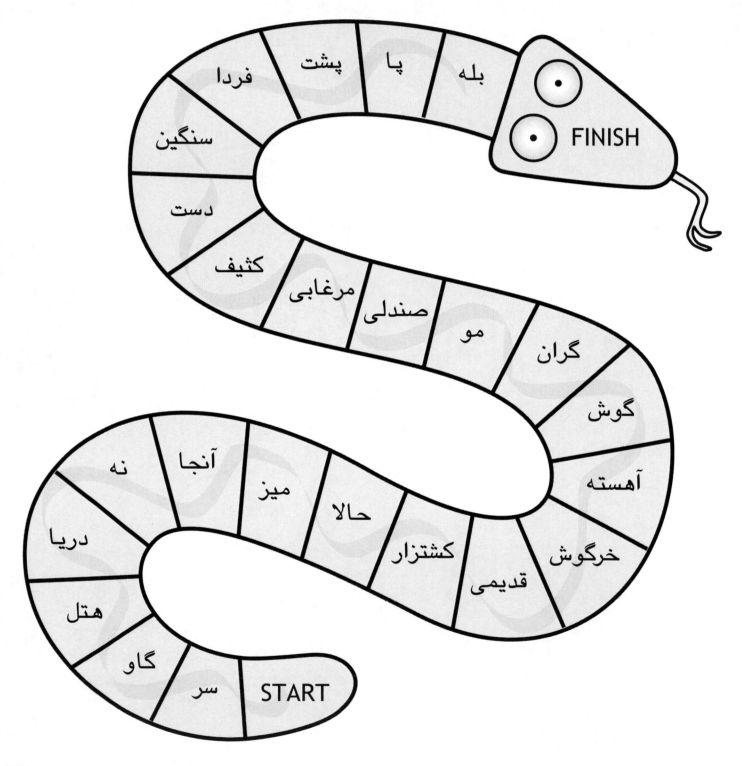

Answers

❶ AROUND THE HOME

Page 10 (top)

See page 9 for correct picture.

Page 10 (bottom)

door	در
cupboard	قفسه
stove	خوراکپز
bed	تخت خواب
table	میز
chair	صَندَلی
refrigerator	یخچال
computer	کامپیوتر

Page 11 (top)

میز	*meez*
قفسه	*ghafaseh*
کامپیوتر	*kaampyooter*
تخت خواب	*takhteh khaab*
پنجره	*panjareh*
تلفن	*telefon*
تلویزیون	*televeezyon*
صَندَلی	*sandalee*

Page 11 (bottom)

گ	ا	ک	ا	پ	و	ف
ط	ی	ص	د	ل	د	ط
ر	د	چ	ل	ز	ت	ه
ه	ب	ق	و	ظ	ف	ه
ر	ف	ک	ل	ا	ل	ی
ت	ط	پ	ب	?	ا	ر
ل	ا	خ	ی	ذ	ف	و
ث	ز	م	ح	پ	ب	ش

Page 12

Page 13

English word: window

❷ CLOTHES

Page 15 (top)

پیراهن زنانه	*peeraahaneh zanaaneh*
شورت	*short*
کفش	*kafsh*
کمربند	*kamarband*
پیراهن مردانه	*peeraahaneh mardaaneh*
تی شرت	*tee shert*
کلاه	*kolaah*
جوراب	*jooraab*

Page 15 (bottom)

ق	ی	ق	ث	ل	پ	ف	ر
ط	ک	ش	ل	و	ا	ر	ط
د	ه	ت	ب	ا	ر	و	چ
ن	م	د	ق	و	ظ	ق	د
ه	م	پ	ا	ل	ت	و	—
ف	ن	ک	ش	ظ	ب	ی	ش
م	ر	و	ل	ا	و	ی	ر
ح	ذ	ا	غ	چ	پ	ف	ث

Page 16

hat	کلاه	*kolaah*
shoe	کفش	*kafsh*
sock	جوراب	*jooraab*
shorts	شورت	*short*
t-shirt	تی شرت	*tee shert*
belt	کمربند	*kamarband*
coat	پالتو	*paalto*
pants	شلوار	*shalvaar*

Page 17

کلاه (hat)	2
پالتو (coat)	0
کمربند (belt)	2
کفش (shoe)	2 (1 pair)
شلوار (pants)	0
شورت (shorts)	2
پیراهن زنانه (dress)	1
جوراب (sock)	6 (3 pairs)
دامن (skirt)	1
تی شرت (t-shirt)	3
پیراهن مردانه (shirt)	0
پولیور (sweater)	1

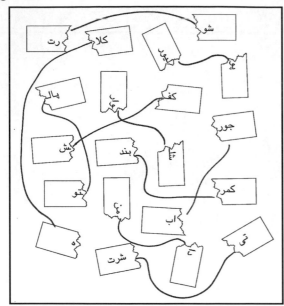

English word: school

Page 23

اتوبوس	*otoboos*
تاکسی	*taaksee*
مدرسه	*madreseh*
ماشین	*maasheen*
هتل	*hotel*
خانه	*khaneh*
دوچرخه	*docharkheh*
قطار	*ghataar*
فروشگاه	*forooshgaah*
سینما	*seenemaa*
رستوران	*restooraan*
جاده	*jaaddeh*

❸ AROUND TOWN

Page 20 (top)

movie theater	سینما
store	فروشگاه
hotel	هتل
taxi	تاکسی
car	ماشین
train	قطار
school	مدرسه
house	خانه

Page 20 (bottom)

bicycle	4
taxi	7
house	2
train	6
bus	1
road	3
car	5

Page 21

❹ COUNTRYSIDE

Page 25

See page 24 for correct picture.

Page 26

پل	✔	کشتزار	✔
درخت	✔	جنگل	✔
بیابان	✘	دریاچه	✘
تپه	✔	رود	✔
کوه	✔	گل	✔
دریا	✘	مزرعه	✔

Page 27 (top)

کوه	*kooh*
رود	*rood*
جنگل	*jangal*
بیابان	*biaabaan*
دریا	*daryaa*
مزرعه	*mazra`eh*
پل	*pol*
کشتزار	*keshtzaar*

مدرسه   تاکسی   اتوبوس

رستوران   قطار   ماشین

هتل   دوچرخه

Page 27 (bottom)

د	ر	ا	و	ل	پ	چ	و	ك
ط	ا	ف	ه	ی	ت	ص	ا
د	د	ز	ت	ز	چ	ر	د
ه	ب	ت	خ	ر	د	و	گ
ه	ف	ی	لا	ا	ك	ذ	ص
پ	ط	د	ر	ا	ی	چ	ه
و	چ	خ	ی	ذ	ف	گ	ل
ف	ز	ه	ع	ر	ز	م	ب

Page 28

sea	دریا	*daryaa*
lake	دریاچه	*daryaacheh*
desert	بیابان	*biaabaan*
farm	مزرعه	*mazra`eh*
flower	گل	*gol*
mountain	کوه	*kooh*
river	رود	*rood*
field	کشتزار	*keshtzaar*

❺ OPPOSITES

Page 30

expensive	گران
big	بزرگ
light	سبک
slow	آهسته
clean	تمیز
inexpensive	ارزان
dirty	کثیف
small	کوچک
heavy	سنگین
new	جدید
fast	تند
old	قدیمی

Page 31

English word: change

Page 32

Odd one outs are those which are not opposites:

سنگین
کوچک
جدید
کثیف
آهسته
ارزان

Page 33

old	جدید
big	کوچک
new	قدیمی
slow	تند
dirty	تمیز
small	بزرگ
heavy	سبک
clean	کثیف
light	سنگین
expensive	ارزان
inexpensive	گران

❻ ANIMALS

Page 35

گاو   خرگوش   ماهی   شیر

گوسفند   سگ   میمون

اسب   موش   گربه

Page 36

خرگوش	*khargoosh*
اسب	*asb*
میمون	*meimoon*
سگ	*sag*
گربه	*gorbeh*
موش	*moosh*
مرغابی	*morghaabee*
ماهی	*maahee*
شیر	*sheer*
گوسفند	*goosfand*
گاو	*gaav*
فیل	*feel*

Page 37

elephant	✔	mouse	✘
monkey	✘	cat	✔
sheep	✔	dog	✘
lion	✔	cow	✔
fish	✔	horse	✘
duck	✘	rabbit	✔

61

Page 38

monkey	میمون
cow	گاو
mouse	موش
dog	سگ
sheep	گوسفند
fish	ماهی
lion	شیر
elephant	فیل
cat	گربه
duck	مرغابی
rabbit	خرگوش
horse	اسب

❼ PARTS OF THE BODY

Page 40

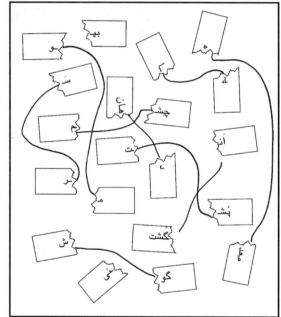

Page 41 (top)

You should have also drawn pictures of:
leg; mouth; ear; nose; eye; hair

62

Page 41 (bottom)

سر	sar
گوش	goosh
معده	me`deh
بینی	beenee
بازو	baazoo
دهان	dahaan
چشم	cheshm
پشت	posht

Page 42

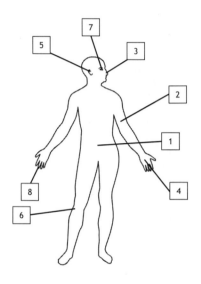

1.	معده	me`deh
2.	بینی	beenee
3.	گوش	goosh
4.	چشم	cheshm
5.	بازو	baazoo
6.	دست	dast
7.	پا	paa
8.	انگشت	angosht

Page 43

ear	گوش	goosh
hair	مو	moo
hand	دست	dast
stomach	معده	me`deh
arm	بازو	baazoo
back	پشت	posht
finger	انگشت	angosht
leg	پا	paa

⑧ USEFUL EXPRESSIONS

Page 45 (top)

great!	عالی!
yes	بله
yesterday	دیروز
where?	کجا؟
today	امروز
here	اینجا
please	لطفا
no	نه

Page 45 (bottom)

آنجا	aanjaa
سلام	salaam
فردا	fardaa
خدا حافظ	khodaa haafez
چند؟	chand?
ممنون	mamnoon
ببخشید	bebakhsheed
عالی!	aalee!

Page 46

English word: please

Page 47

Page 48

yes	بله	baleh
hello	سلام	salaam
no	نه	na
sorry	ببخشید	bebakhsheed
please	لطفا	lotfan
there	آنجا	aanjaa
thank you	ممنون	mamnoon
tomorrow	فردا	fardaa

● ROUND-UP

Page 49

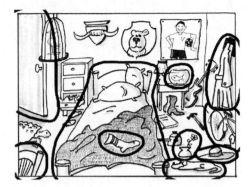

Page 50

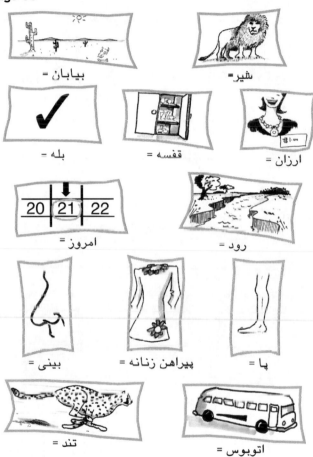

Page 51

میز (Because it isn't an animal.)

تلفن (Because it isn't a means of transportation.)

کشتزار (Because it isn't an item of clothing.)

درخت (Because it isn't connected with water.)

سینما (Because it isn't a descriptive word.)

ماهی (Because it lives in water/doesn't have legs.)

کاناپه (Because it isn't a part of the body.)

لطفاً (Because it isn't an expression of time.)

تخت خواب (Because you wouldn't find it in the kitchen.)

Page 52

Words that appear in the picture:

تی شرت
ماشین
گل
کفش
قطار
میمون
تلویزیون
صندلی
کمربند
شورت

Page 53

sweater	پولیور	*buloofir*
lake	دریاچه	*daryaacheh*
thank you	ممنون	*mamnoon*
bed	تخت خواب	*takhteh khaab*
house	خانه	*khaaneh*
forest	جنگل	*jangal*
where?	کجا؟	*kojaa?*
heavy	سنگین	*sangeen*

Page 54

English phrase: well done!

Page 55

شورت	✔ (shade)
تی شرت	✘
در	✔ (handle)
گربه	✘
صندلی	✔ (back)
ماهی	✔ (direction)
جوراب	✔ (pattern)
سگ	✘

Page 56

refrigerator	یخچال
pants	شلوار
store	فروشگاه
school	مدرسه
river	رود
great!	عالی!
small	کوچک
light	سبک
arm	بازو
stomach	معده
clean	تمیز
horse	اسب

Page 57

سلام	*salaam*
دیروز	*deerooz*
خوراکپز	*khoraakpaz*
سینما	*seenemaa*
تاکسی	*taaksee*
کوه	*kooh*
کشتزار	*keshtzaar*
بزرگ	*bozorg*
جدید	*jadeed*
گوسفند	*goosfand*
انگشت	*angosht*
فیل	*feel*

Page 58

Here are the English equivalents and pronunciation of the words, in order from START to FINISH:

head *sar*	farm *mazra`eh*	duck *morghaabee*
cow *gaav*	old *ghadeemee*	dirty *kaseef*
hotel *hotel*	rabbit *khargoosh*	hand *dast*
sea *daryaa*	slow *aahesteh*	heavy *sangeen*
no *na*	ear *goosh*	tomorrow *fardaa*
there *aanjaa*	expensive *geraan*	back *posht*
table *meez*	hair *moo*	leg *paa*
now *haalaa*	chair *sandalee*	yes *baleh*

کامپیوتر

kaampyooter

پنجره

panjareh

میز

meez

قفسه

ghafaseh

یخچال

yakhchaal

صندلی

sandalee

کاناپه

kaanaapeh

خوراکپز

khoraakpaz

در

dar

تخت خواب

takhteh khaab

تلفن

telefon

تلویزیون

televeezyon

window	computer
cupboard	table
chair	refrigerator
stove	sofa
bed	door
television	telephone

کمربند *kamarband*	پالتو *paalto*
دامن *daaman*	کلاه *kolaah*
تی شرت *tee shert*	کفش *kafsh*
پولیور *poleever*	پیراهن مردانه *peeraahaneh mardaaneh*
شورت *short*	جوراب *jooraab*
شلوار *shalvaar*	پیراهن زنانه *peeraahaneh zanaaneh*

coat	belt
shoe	t-shirt
hat	skirt
shirt	sweater
sock	shorts
dress	pants

مدرسه

madreseh

ماشین

maasheen

جاده

jaaddeh

سینما

seenemaa

هتل

hotel

فروشگاه

forooshgaah

تاکسی

taaksee

دوچرخه

docharkheh

رستوران

restooraan

اتوبوس

otoboos

قطار

ghataar

خانه

khaaneh

car	school
movie theater	road
store	hotel
bicycle	taxi
bus	restaurant
house	train

دریاچه

daryaacheh

جنگل

jangal

تپه

tappeh

دریا

daryaa

کوه

kooh

درخت

derakht

بیابان

biaabaan

گل

gol

پل

pol

رود

rood

مزرعه

mazra`eh

کشتزار

keshtzaar

forest	lake
sea	hill
tree	mountain
flower	desert
river	bridge
field	farm

سنگین

sangeen

سبک

sabok

بزرگ

bozorg

کوچک

koochek

قدیمی

ghadeemee

جدید

jadeed

تند

tond

آهسته

aahestch

تمیز

tameez

کثیف

kaseef

ارزان

arzaan

گران

geraan

light	heavy
small	big
new	old
slow	fast
dirty	clean
expensive	inexpensive

مرغابی

morghaabee

گربه

gorbeh

موش

moosh

گاو

gaav

خرگوش

khargoosh

سگ

sag

اسب

asb

میمون

meimoon

شیر

sheer

ماهی

maahee

فیل

feel

گوسفند

goosfand

cat	duck
cow	mouse
dog	rabbit
monkey	horse
fish	lion
sheep	elephant

بازو

baazoo

انگشت

angosht

سر

sar

دهان

dahaan

گوش

goosh

پا

paa

دست

dast

معده

me`deh

چشم

cheshm

مو

moo

بینی

beenee

پشت

posht

finger	arm
mouth	head
leg	ear
stomach	hand
hair	eye
back	nose

لطفاً

lotfan

ممنون

mamnoon

بله

baleh

نه

na

سلام

salaam

خدا حافظ

khodaa haafez

دیروز

deerooz

امروز

emrooz

فردا

fardaa

کجا؟

kojaa?

اینجا

eenjaa

آنجا

aanjaa

ببخشید!

bebakhsheed!

چند؟

chand?

عالی!

aalee!

حالا

haalaa

thank you	please
no	yes
goodbye	hello
today	yesterday
where?	tomorrow
there	here
how much?	sorry!
now	great!